Scottish Jokes

SCOTTISH JOKES

Edited by Chris Findlater

WAVERLEY BOOKS

Compiled by RLS Ltd

© 1998 Waverley Books Ltd,
David Dale House,
New Lanark, ML11 9DJ

Illustrations by Jim Barker

First published 1998
Reprinted 1999, 2000, 2002

ISBN 1 84205 169 5

Printed and bound in the UK

A Texan visitor to Aberdeenshire was visiting a farm to see the bulls.

"How many acres have you got?" he asked.

"Two thousand," said the farmer.

"Is that all? I can get in my car and drive all day and still not reach my boundary fence."

"I sympathise," said the farmer. "I had a car like that once."

Two little boys shouted at the minister, "Hey, mister, the Devil's deid."

"In that case," he answered, "I must pray for two fatherless bairns."

A keen Scottish rugby supporter was watching a match against England at Murrayfield. Beside him was the only empty seat in the entire stadium.

"Whose seat is that?" asked the man on the other side.

"It's my wife's."

"But why isn't she here?"

"She's dead."

"Well, why didn't you give the ticket to one of your friends?"

"They're all at the funeral."

Another minister was walking along the road when he saw two little girls playing in the dirt.

"What are you making?" he asked kindly.

"We're making a church," said one of the girls.

"How nice. And has your church got a minister?"

"There's no' enough dirt to make a minister," said the other little girl.

A man from Aberdeen came across a perfectly good crutch lying by the side of the road. He picked it up, hurried home with it and broke his wife's leg.

A Morayshire tramp had found a good wheeze to get food from farmers' wives. He knocked at the door, holding a piece of dried-up cowpat, and asked for a crust of bread to eat with it. The horrified ladies always made him throw away the cowpat and gave him a good meal. But at one house, the farmer himself answered the door. The tramp held up the cowpat and made his usual request. The farmer was shocked.

"Man, you can't eat that!" he said. "Come roond to the yaird wi' me and I'll find you a nice, hot, fresh one."

Notice on Scottish golf club wall:
Rule No 979: A ball cannot be picked up as lost at least until it has stopped rolling.

Sir Harry Lauder was strolling in Dundee one dark night when he saw a man grubbing about on his hands and knees.

"What are you looking for?" asked the great comedian.

"My ear," said the man. "I've just been in a bit of a scrap."

"What a vicious fellow the other man must have been," said Sir Harry. "Would you know him again if you saw him?"

"I think so," was the answer. "I have his nose in my pocket."

The minister's son from a Highland village had been a bit of a teenage tearaway and a source of worry to his parents. When it was time for him to go away to university in Aberdeen, they were anxious about the effect on him of life in the city.

But he promised to reform and work hard. Regular letters came back to say how hard he was working, how many lectures he was attending, and so on. His father was so pleased that he determined to pay his son a visit to tell him how glad he was. It took him a long time to drive to Aberdeen, and it was well into the evening, and dark, when he knocked on the door of his son's lodgings. An upstairs window went up and the landlady's head poked out.

"What is it?" she asked.

"Does Willie Lamond live here?" asked the minister.

"Aye, he does. Just carry him in," replied the lady.

"**I**'ve kissed every woman in this tenement block except one," said an amorous Glaswegian to his friend, just as one of the male residents of the block was passing. The man immediately turned back, went upstairs and reported this to his wife.

"I wonder who the woman is that this rascal hasn't kissed?" he said.

"Oh," said his wife, "I suppose it'll be that stuck-up Mary Mackintosh on the third floor."

What's the difference between a wedding and a wake in Scotland?

There's one drunk less at a wake.

Two lads from the West Coast got jobs at a sawmill. On the very first morning, one called out to the other, "Hey, Donald, I've lost a finger!"

"How did you you do that?"

"I just tried it against this round, spinning thing here – damn it, there goes another one!"

How do you get a Highlander onto the roof?
Tell him that the drinks are on the house.

Two men were sitting drinking side by side at a bar in Glasgow. After Jack the barman had served them several whiskies, one suddenly turned to the other and said, "Where are you from?"

"From the Isle of Mull," replied the other.

"Is that so? So am I. This deserves a drink." And he ordered two large ones. "Where abouts on Mull?"

"From Tobermory."

"Tobermory? Me too."

"Well, that calls for a dram." And the other ordered two more large ones. "What street did you live on?"

"Harbour Street."

"This is amazing. I grew up on Harbour Street."

"Fancy, after all that, us meeting like this in the middle of Glasgow."

One of the regulars wandered into the pub.

"How are things, Jack?" he asked the barman. "Och, the same as usual. The wife's giving trouble, the landlord's mean as ever. Oh, and the Maclean twins are plastered again."

Before the bridge to Skye was built, a ferry operated. One day a man on a bicycle came pedalling down the street of Kyle of Lochalsh in a great hurry to catch the ferry. As he came to the waterfront, he saw the vessel was ten yards from the jetty. Seeing a plank laid at an angle on a herring-box, he steered on to it, soared into the air, and was just able to grab the side of the boat. Hauling his bike over the rails, he said to a crewman,

"Phew! That was a close thing."

"Actually," said the crewman, "this ferry's on the way in."

Red Adair, the Texan oil-fire fighter, walked into a bar in Aberdeen one evening. The man next to him at the bar immediately spotted him as an American.

"I've been to the States myself," he said.

"Oh, really," said the Texan, in a tired voice.

"Oh, yes, I was in California a whole month. I went to a concert with a famous country singer called Benny Rogers, and . . ."

"Would that be Kenny Rogers?"

"Oh, yes. That's right. And he sang with a woman with a fine figure, Polly Darton."

"Do you mean Dolly Parton?"

The American's voice was terse, and the man decided it was time to change the subject.

"Have I not seen you on the TV?" he asked.

"Maybe. I'm Red Adair."

"What! Red Adair? I must have your autograph. And are you still married to Ginger Rogers?"

Two lady teachers from a remote part of Scotland went on holiday to London together. Walking in the West End they saw a hot-dog stand. Feeling they ought to try everything, they each ordered a hot dog. When she received hers, Miss Macphail looked doubtfully at it and asked Miss MacAlister, "Which part of the dog did *you* get, Hughina?"

Why do pipers march when they play? A moving target is harder to hit.

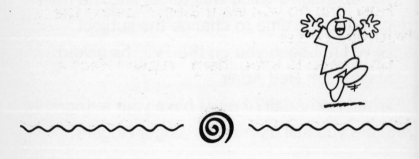

Hector and his smarter brother Hamish were building a shed. Hamish noticed that Hector was throwing away about half of the nails.

"Why are you throwing these away?" he asked.

"They're pointing the wrong way," said Hector.

Hamish thought about this for a while, then he said, "Keep them. They'll do for knocking in on the other side."

In the end Hector had to go and buy some more nails.

"How long do you want them?" asked the hardware dealer.

"Oh, I need to keep them," replied Hector.

How does a Moray ploughman have a bubble bath?

He has a plate of beans for dinner.

A performing arts group from the south went on tour in Argyll. One day, one of the actors rang his girlfriend in Glasgow.

"How's it going?" she asked.

"Terrible," he said. "Last night we had two sheep in the hall."

"What did the audience say?"

"They were the audience."

The Waverley Steps in Edinburgh are famous for their updraught of wind, even on summer days. A lady commuter, feeling her skirt swirl up as she reached the top of the steps, glared angrily at a man loitering there.

"Do you mind?" she said icily.

"Aye, I mind fine," he said, with a leer. "You had the same pair on yesterday."

A border rugby referee died and went to Heaven. At the gate he met Saint Peter who asked if he had carried out any action where principles went ahead of self-interest.

"Well," said the man, "I was reffing a game between Hawick and Jedburgh. Hawick were two points ahead, with two minutes to go. The Jed wing made a break, and passed inside to his lock. The lock was driven on by his forwards, passed out to the flanker who ducked blind and went over in the corner. However, the flanker dropped the ball before he could ground it. Since Hawick had played a better game all through, I ruled that he had dropped the ball down, not forward, and awarded the try."

"That was quite brave," said Saint Peter. "Let me just check it in the book."

He consulted his huge tome, then closed it with a snap.

"There's nothing in the book about it," he said. "When did it happen?"

"Forty-five seconds ago," said the ref.

Golf – the sport in which you shout "Fore!", shoot five, and write three.

A high-rise building was going up in central Glasgow, and three steel erectors sat on a girder having their lunch.

"Oh, no, not cream cheese and walnut again," said the first, who came from Coatbridge. "If I get the same again tomorrow, I'll jump off the girder."

The second, who came from Airdrie, opened his packet.

"Oh, no, not a Caesar salad with salami and lettuce on rye," he said. "If I get the same again tomorrow, I'll jump off too."

The third man, who came from Dufftown, opened his lunch.

"Oh, no, not another potato sandwich," he said. "If I get the same again tomorrow, I'll follow you chaps off the girder."

The next day, the Coatbridge man got cream cheese and walnut. Without delay, he jumped. The Airdrie man saw he had Caesar salad with salami and lettuce on rye. With a wild cry, he leapt into eternity. The Dufftown man then opened his lunchbox.

"Oh, no," he said. "Potato sandwiches." And he too jumped.

The foreman, who had overheard their conversation, reported what had happened, and the funerals were held together.

"If only I'd known," sobbed the wife of the Coatbridge man.

"If only he'd said," wailed the wife of the Airdrie man.

"I don't understand it at all," said the wife of the Dufftown man. "He always got his own sandwiches ready."

Hector and his smarter brother Hamish were running a ferry service to one of the Hebridean islands. One day it was particularly stormy and the boat was tossed about on the waves.

"We'll sink, we'll sink!" wailed Hector.

"Quick, then, get roond and collect the fares," shouted Hamish. "Otherwise we'll all be drooned before they've paid."

Dr Watson of Edinburgh was famous for his bedside manner and his ability to reassure patients. Calling on one of his patients one day, he said, "I have bad news and very bad news. Which would you like me to tell you first?"

The patient gulped. "Er, the bad news, Doctor."

"You have only one day left to live," said Dr Watson.

"If that's the bad news, what can the very bad news be?" gasped the patient.

"I should have told you yesterday."

Andy Macmillan, the barman, had a new customer who was very regular in his habits. Every day he would come into the pub and order three drams of whisky. He would raise each one ceremoniously and drink it down. After a while, Andy asked him why he did it that way.

"It's like this," said the man. "I have two brothers. One lives in Manitoba and the other in Queensland. We never see each other, but we have this way of drinking: we each have one for ourselves and one for each of the other two, and that way we feel we're still in touch."

But one day the man came in and ordered only two whiskies. He drank them down in the usual way and was about to go when Andy said, "I hope nothing's happened to one of your brothers."

"No, no," said the man. "They're both fine."

"But you only had the two nips," said Andy.

"Oh, I see what you mean," said the man. "The thing is, you see, I've given up drinking."

MacTavish, charged with stealing a Porsche, angrily protested his innocence, and his advocate got him acquitted. The next day, he turned up at the police station.

"I want you to run in that lawyer of mine," he said.

"But why?" said the inspector. "He got you off, didn't he?"

"Aye, but I didn't pay him, and now he's gone and took that car I stole."

The boy on the work-experience scheme was sent off with a painter. When they arrived at the place of work they parked at the back. The painter gave the lad a pot of red paint and a brush.

"I'll give you an easy job," he said. "Go round to the front and paint the porch."

In about an hour the boy returned.

"Have you finished it already?" asked the painter.

"Yes. But it's not a Porsche, it's a BMW."

A couple from the north east were watching the National Lottery results on television while they worked at the kitchen table.

"Hey, Tammas, it's our numbers!" shouted his wife. "We've won ten million pounds."

"Okay, okay, but just finish off today's begging letters," he said.

Robert the Bruce, as everybody knows, was hiding in a cave when he saw a spider swinging on its thread, trying to reach the cave wall. Several times it tried, and failed, as the fugitive king sat watching. Then, at last, it succeeded. What the official legend does not record is that it then turned to Bruce and said, in complaining tones, "I could have done it the very first time, but I just hate doing it when anyone's watching me."

Actually, the spider was taking part in a thread-swinging competition. When it finally swung to the cave wall, the other spiders angrily disqualified it.

"I saw him blowing you," said the chief judge.

Later, when Bruce and the spider had got friendly, they went to a tavern together. Bruce, in disguise, ordered a large whisky and three flies for the spider. The spider ate one fly and then decided it wasn't very hungry and wrapped the other two up in its silk thread to take away. As they were about to leave, Bruce noticed that the threads had worked loose.

"Hey," he said, "You can't go out like that. Your flies are undone."

On the train from Edinburgh to Perth, the ticket collector was having a fierce argument with a passenger who had no ticket. The passenger claimed that she was a schoolgirl entitled to a half-fare, though to the ticket collector she looked somewhat older. She had a big brown hold-all on her knees. In the end her rudeness so annoyed the official that he picked up the hold-all just as the train was going over the Forth Bridge and threatened to throw it out of the window.

"That's right!" shouted the passenger. "You men are all the same. First you refuse to believe I'm still at school, then you threaten to throw my little boy into the sea."

The only plumber in Glasgow to charge reasonable fees died and was sent to Hell by mistake. Eventually it was realised in Heaven that there was an honest plumber in the wrong place. Saint Peter telephoned on the hot line to Satan.

"Have you got an honest plumber there?"

"Yes."

"He's ours, can you send him up?"

"You can't have him."

"Why not?"

"Because he's the only one who understands air conditioning. It's really cool down here now, man."

"Send him up," shouted Saint Peter, "or we'll sue."

"You'll sue?" laughed the voice at the other end. "And where will you get hold of a lawyer?"

As a Christmas present one year, the laird gave his gamekeeper, MacPhail, a deerstalker hat with ear-flaps. MacPhail was most appreciative and always wore it with the flaps tied under his chin to keep his ears warm in the winter winds. Then one cold, windy day the laird noticed he wasn't wearing the hat.

"Where's the hat?" he asked.

"I've given up wearing it since the accident," was the reply.

"Accident? I didn't know you'd had an accident."

"A man offered me a nip of whisky, and I had the earflaps down and never heard him."

A ventriloquist was driving to a show when his car broke down near a farmhouse. He walked up to the farm to ask if he could make a telephone call to the nearest garage. When he had done so, he walked back through the farmyard with the farmer. As they passed the horse's stall, the ventriloquist said to the horse, "Hello, how are you today?"

"Fine," said the horse. "The farmer here gives me plenty of oats."

The farmer gasped, but the ventriloquist walked on, smiling. When they came to the byre, a cow was looking out.

"How are you today?" asked the ventriloquist.

"Fine", said the cow. "The farmer here makes excellent silage."

The farmer stared at the cow in amazement. They strolled on and came to a sheep-pen. The farmer suddenly turned to the ventriloquist and grasped his arm.

"Don't believe a word that sheep says. It's the biggest liar for miles around."

What do you call six weeks of rain in Fort William?
  The summer holidays.

Hector and Hamish went to the pictures to see a film that had a horse race in it.

"I bet that black one will win," said Hamish.

"I bet he won't," said Hector.

The black horse won, and then Hamish admitted he'd seen the film before.

"I saw it too," said Hector. "But I thought he would never win two times in a row."

A woman with a baby in her arms got onto a bus in Dunfermline. As she put her money into the cash machine, the driver said, "That's the ugliest baby I've ever seen."

The woman was so astonished she did not react, but went and sat down. Then she said to the man sitting across the aisle, "That driver is the rudest man I've ever met."

"Tut, tut," said the man sympathetically.

"I've a good mind to go and get his name so that I can complain."

"Yes, go on, hen," said the man. "I'll hold your monkey for you while you do it."

The elderly man was reminiscing to his young grandchildren about his wartime experiences with a Scottish regiment.

"Yes," he said, "I fought in Africa, Italy and Germany. I fought with Montgomery, I fought with Wavell and I fought with Alexander."

"Couldn't you get on with anybody, Grandpa?" asked his granddaughter.

An actors' company was touring Scotland with a deeply unsuccessful play about the life of Napoleon. The worst moment came at a matinée in Perth, with only a handful of people in the theatre. The leading actor had taken to drinking, and when his colleague, dressed as the captain of HMS *Bellerophon*, said, "We are taking you to St Helena," he blurted out, "Take me anywhere you like, so long as it isn't Perth."

Bagpipes – defined as the missing link between music and noise.

The new receptionist in a Highland hotel was very surprised when the young man in Room 8 came down late at night and gave her an extra big smile. Then he came round the desk and put his arm round her.

"Excuse me," she said. "How dare you?"

"It's in the Bible," said the young man. Then he kissed her.

"Really, that's enough," she said, struggling free.

"But it's in the Bible," repeated the young man.

"What do you mean, it's in the Bible?" she asked, indignantly.

"I'll show you," he said. He rushed up to his room and returned with the Gideon Bible. He opened it at the flyleaf where someone had written, "The receptionist's a pushover."

The MacPhindoe family from Glasgow had come up rapidly in the world and had moved out to a big new house in Bearsden. Mrs MacPhindoe decided they should go to the opera and rang up for tickets.

"Is that two tickets for Madame Butterfly?" asked the voice at the other end.

"No, no, for Mrs MacPhindoe."

Whilst they were shopping in Glasgow's finest department store, Mr MacPhindoe saw a diamond tiara.

"Will we buy you a coronet, Maggie?" he said.

"Don't be stupid," said his wife. "You know I can't play any musical instrument."

A passer-by outside a small Highland village saw a young girl struggling to drive a reluctant cow along the road.

"I've got to take it out to the bull," explained the child.

"Couldn't your father do that?" asked the passer-by.

"Oh, no," said the child. "He said it had to be the bull."

Hector and Hamish rented a boat to go out fishing on a loch. To their surprise, they both caught several big trout.

"We must come back to this place," said Hamish. "Leave a wee marker so we'll find it again."

Hector bent down and marked a big X on the boards of the boat.

"There," he said proudly.

"That's no good," shouted Hamish. "What if they give us another boat next time?"

A music lover was on his way to a concert in the Usher Hall in Edinburgh when he lost his way. Seeing a man hurrying along with a cello case, he ran up and said, "Excuse me, can you tell me how I can get to the Usher Hall?"

The other paused, glared at him for a moment, and said, "Practise, man. Practise."

Unsuccessful golfer to caddie:

"You must be the worst caddie in the entire world."

Caddie to golfer:

"That would be just too much of a coincidence."

A Scots sailor was shipwrecked and washed ashore on a tropical island. As he opened his eyes and gazed around, he saw a lovely young woman wearing only a grass skirt.

"Are you hungry?" she murmured.

"Very," he groaned. She reached into a little bag woven from palm leaves and brought out a pie and chips wrapped in the previous day's *Evening News* and still hot. He ate with gusto.

"Are you thirsty?"

"Very," he groaned, more hopefully. From the little bag she produced a bottle of fine old single malt whisky, and he took a long, contented swig.

"And now," she said, nestling against him, "how would you like to play around?"

The Scotsman sat up in delighted amazement.

"Don't tell me you've got a set of golf clubs in there!" he cried.

A group of Boy Scouts from England went camping in the West Highlands. As the sun went down on the first day, the midges appeared and swarmed around, biting and tickling despite everything the lads could do to stop them. As it grew darker, some glow-worms appeared.

"It's not fair!" shouted a harassed tenderfoot. "They've got searchlight support."

Two Banffshire farmworkers were shifting a trailer-load of manure out of the farmyard. Without looking, the tractor driver swung out blithely into the roadway. A Ferrari, approaching at high speed, was forced to brake violently, swerved through the gate into the farmyard, hit a wall and burst into flames.

"Didja see that?" cried the tractor driver. "We got oota there jist in the nick o' time!"

Enjoying a round of golf with a distant acquaintance, I saw him sink a twenty-foot putt on the first green with a grunt of satisfaction. His little dog, which had come with us, promptly stood up on his back legs and uttered a shrill "Yip, yip."

"That's remarkable," I said. "What does he do if you miss your putt?"

"He turns somersaults," said my friend.

"Oh, really! How many?"

"Depends on how hard I kick him."

A Scotsman and an Englishman were in the jungle together. Suddenly, a lion appeared in the distance. The Scotsman immediately pulled off his heavy boots and started to put on a pair of trainers.

"What's the use of that?" said the Englishman. "You'll never outrun a lion."

"No, but I'll outrun you," said the Scotsman.

A man went into one of the many pubs in Rose Street, Edinburgh, and ran an eye over the huge selection of malt whiskies on display.

"I'll have a dram of that, and that, and that, and that," he said, pointing.

The barman duly set four glasses in front of him. With great speed the man drained each glass in turn.

"You were in a hurry," commented the barman.

"So would you be if you had what I have," said the man.

"Oh, what's that?" asked the barman in a sympathetic tone.

"Nae money," said the man.

When his sheepdog died, Mr McMeikle the farmer was very distressed. He went to the parish priest and said, "Father, will you do a funeral for my dog?"

"I certainly will not," said the priest. "Why don't you try the minister?"

"All right," said the farmer. "By the way, do you think a thousand pounds for his church fund would be a suitable gesture of gratitude?"

"Wait a minute," said the priest. "Why didn't you mention that the dog was a Catholic?"

On the roof above Central Station in Glasgow, a young pigeon was being educated by its parent.

"Noo, d'ye ken whit ye're supposed tae dae?" said the grown-up pigeon.

"I think so," said the little one.

"Off ye go and try oot yer style then."

The little pigeon wobbled off the ledge and flew down towards the station entrance. Selecting a man in a bowler hat, it landed with a great flapping of wings on his hat and clung on desperately despite the man's efforts to beat it off. After a while it gave up and flew back up to the roof.

"How wiz zat?" it asked.

"Terrible, terrible," said its parent. "Ye didnae listen tae a word. Watch me."

Off it flew and expertly dive-bombed a lady getting out of a taxi. Then it flew up again.

"D'ye see noo?"

"Oh, I see," said the little pigeon. "I thought ye wiz saying '*Sit* on their heids.'"

"I can never get my coffee to taste right," moaned Angus. "It's always too bitter or too sweet."

"How is that?"

"I like it with two lumps of sugar, you see."

"Well, then?"

"Well, when I'm at home, I just put the one lump in to be economical. And when I'm out, I always take the chance to put three in."

A Lewisman, planning a visit to Glasgow, telephoned the airline to ask how long the flight from Stornoway took.

"Just one second, sir," said the lady at the other end.

"Thanks very much," he said, and hung up.

Mrs MacPhindoe, of the newly rich family from Glasgow, called in an interior designer to advise on the decoration and furnishing of their big new house. As they went from room to room, he was surprised that in every room at the back of the house she opened the window, and called out, "Green sides up! Green sides up!"

Baffled by this, he finally asked, "Are you a football supporter or something?"

"Oh, no," said Mrs MacPhindoe. "It's just I've got my two nephews from Partick laying turf for me in the back garden."

Dr Watson had a patient who was both self-important and boring. One day, whilst a minor complaint was being dealt with, the patient said, "I've been invited to speak to the Rotary Club next week. The question is, what should I tell them?"

"Tell them you've got flu," said Dr Watson.

Thomas and Tillie had been married for some time and had spent a lot of it arguing and losing their tempers, with Tillie retiring upstairs and Thomas retiring to the pub. One day, prompted by a friend, Thomas went to see a marriage guidance counsellor.

"I'd need to see you together," said the counsellor, "but I will tell you one thing. A woman likes to feel loved and appreciated. Why not try telling her you love her? You'll find you feel better too."

Thomas looked rather doubtful as he left. However, during the day he resolved to try out the advice. He came straight home from work.

"How's your day been, Tillie?" he asked benevolently.

"Don't ask," she said. "There's been a power cut, the children have broken my best bowl, the cat's been sick on the bed...."

He put his arm round her.

"Never mind, Tillie, your Thomas loves you," he said.

She pushed him away with a violent shove.

"And to cap it all, you come home drunk!" she shouted.

Bring your golf ball to be re-covered. –
Advertisement in Aberdeen.

"**I**'ve given up smoking," said Angus.

"Very good," said his friend. "What was it persuaded you?"

"It's too painful."

"Painful?"

"Aye, I've had my fingers trodden on three times this week so far."

A schoolboy was trying on his first long trousers.

"They're too tight," he said to his mother. "Tighter than my skin."

"How can they be tighter than your skin?"

"I can sit down in my skin."

After an open-air service, the preacher passed his hat round the scanty collection of people who had stood listening to him. It came back completely empty. The preacher raised his eyebrows, surveyed the gathering, then looked skyward.

"I thank Thee, O Lord," he declared, "for the safe return of my hat."

After his barn burned down, a Buchan farmer put in an insurance claim. The agent who came round to inspect the damage and settle the claim tried to sell him some more insurance.

"Are you covered against cattle theft? And what about floods?"

"Floods, eh?" said the farmer. "That's interesting. How do you set about starting a flood?"

Camden, South Carolina, is well known as a Scottish enclave of the USA. It was there that fourteen suicides occurred on the same day. The funeral parlour had put an announcement in the window: Bargains in Coffins, Today Only.

A young couple from the Isle of Mull went to Edinburgh to be married by the registrar.

"Your name?" he asked the man.

"Donald Maclean."

"And yours?" he asked the girl.

"Shona MacLean."

"Any connection?"

Shona blushed bright red.

"Only once," she said, "and we was engaged already."

"Mary's been offered a job working in the Cold Store," said her mother.

"That's nice," said her friend.

"No, no, I made her turn it down. It was too cruel, poor lassie!"

"Too cruel?"

"Yes, they said she had to work in short shifts."

A famous Scottish judge was playing whist partnered by a lady of great refinement but little skill at cards. At one point the lady played quite the wrong card. The judge glowered across the table.

"Ye silly auld bitch," he muttered. Then he realised she had heard him.

"I beg your pardon, ma'am," he said. "For a moment, I mistook ye for my wife."

Why do all Scots have a sense of humour? Because it's a free gift.

After discovering they had won £15,000,000 in the Lottery, Mr and Mrs MacKemble sat down to discuss their future.

"After twenty years of washing other people's stairs," said Mrs MacKemble, "I can throw my old scrubbing brush away at last."

"Of course you can, hen," said her husband. "We can easily afford you a new one now."

A pigeon from George Square in Glasgow was boasting to one from Central Station.

"Whit's yur score rate?" it asked.

"Oh, I dinna ken. Aboot wan in three mebbe. They've tooken tae runnin' lately."

"Huh!" said the first. "Doon in George Square I hit seven oota ten, nae bother."

"That's nae great shakes," said the other. "If I had all them big-heided cooncillors strollin' in and oot o' the City Chambers, I'd get ten oota ten every time."

When Sanders MacGillivray came back from his first trip to London, everyone in the village was keen to find out how he had got on.

"Did you like it?"

"Oh, it was no' bad."

"As good as that, was it?"

"Well, there was just the one thing wrong. The people in my hotel just would not go to their bed. They were outside my room in the corridor shouting and banging till three o'clock in the morning."

"What did you do, Sanders?"

"Och, I just kept on playing my bagpipes."

Three Scotsmen were in jail in Arabia. One was from Edinburgh, one was from Glasgow and one was from Moray. One day the man from Edinburgh found an old brass lamp in a corner of the cell. He rubbed it and a genie appeared.

"Master, I can grant you three wishes."

"Well, there are three of us, can we have one wish each?"

"Most assuredly, O Master."

"Well, I want back to Edinburgh."

And with that, he vanished.

"And I want back to Glasgow," said the Glaswegian. He too vanished.

Only the Moray man was left. He scratched his head.

"I can't make up my mind whether to go back to my mother in Dufftown or my girlfriend in Craigellachie," he said. "I wish my pals were still here to help me decide."

And in a flash, they were.

The Highland Games were on in Blair Atholl and a man of 81 came to toss the caber.

"Don't you think you're a bit old?" said the stewards.

"Not at all, not at all. My father was coming too, but he had to go to my grandfather's wedding to be best man."

"How old is your grandfather?"

"Och, he's a hundred and twenty-four."

"Fancy a man of that age wanting to get married," said a steward.

"Och, he didna want to. He had to," said the man.

A boy aged about ten strolled into a Glasgow pub.

"I'll have a nip and a chaser," he said to the barmaid.

"You'll get me into trouble," said the barmaid.

"We'll get on to that later. First, the drinks," said the boy.

A salesman from another country was making a pitch to the furniture buyer of a Glasgow department store.

"And if you carry our new line of dining suites, I'll have the pleasure of presenting you personally with a case of fine wine," the salesman said.

"Oh, we're not allowed to accept gifts," said the buyer. "That would be a form of bribery."

"I'll tell you what," said the salesman. "Just to keep it all above board, I'll sell you the wine."

"How much for?"

"Say, a pound for the case."

"Oh, well," said the buyer, writing out the purchase order. "At that price, I'll take two cases."

An Australian entered a bar and stood beside a Scotsman.

"Where are you from, pal?" asked the Scotsman, after they'd chatted for a while.

"I'm from the finest country in the whole wide world," said the Australian.

"Are you?" said the other. "You have a damn funny accent for a Scotsman."

When Hamish left home, his mother sent him a woolly cardigan that she had knitted. "Dear son," she wrote, "to save weight and postage, I have cut the buttons off. You'll find them in a little bag in the right-hand pocket."

Hector and Hamish went into their local pub in great good humour and ordered two large whiskies.

"Are you lads celebrating something?" asked the barman.

"We certainly are," said Hector. "We've just finished a jigsaw puzzle in record time. A hundred pieces it had, and it only took us six months."

"Six months? But that's quite a long while," said the barman.

"Not at all," said Hamish. "It said on the box, three to five years."

A team of farm boys from Moray decided to climb Ben Nevis. They borrowed a van load of equipment and set off. Unfortunately, they only got about forty feet up before they ran out of scaffolding.

Two great football fanatics, Andy and Stevie, were discussing the chances of football being played in Heaven. They couldn't see how any self-respecting Heaven would not have football – but yet, they weren't quite sure. Finally they agreed that the one who died first would come back and tell the other if they played football in Heaven or not.

Not long afterwards, Andy was run over by a bus and killed. On the night after the funeral, when Stevie was asleep, a vision of Andy appeared to him. Andy was wearing a long white robe, but Stevie noticed immediately that he had football boots on.

"So they do play football there!" he exclaimed, sitting up in bed.

"Yes," said the vision. "But do you want the good news first or the bad news?"

"Oh, the good news."

"The good news is they have the most fantastic football sides here. There's more footballers here than you might think. And the angels love the game too. We play in the Heavenly League."

"Well, that's great," said Stevie. "What can the bad news be?"

"The bad news is I saw your name on the board for next Sunday's game."

A side in the local amateur league had just acquired a new player of great energy and ferocity but little else. In his first game against the team from the neighbouring town, the new player ran up against its captain, a small, balding, red-haired figure who neatly snaffled the ball from him. It happened again. And again. Losing his temper when it happened a fourth time, he muttered, "If you do that again, I'll bite your head off."

"Do that," said the other, "then you'll have more brains in your belly than you've got in your head."

Jimmy MacDaid was walking across a bridge of the Clyde when he saw a man climb up onto the parapet.

"Ah'm gonna jump," said the man.

"Oh, don't do that," said Jimmy. "Think of your family."

"I dinna have a family."

"Well, think of Rangers."

"I dinna support Rangers."

"Well, think of Celtic then."

"I dinna support Celtic either."

At this the sympathetic Glaswegian gave up.

"Jump then, ye bloody atheist!"

When Hamish was still at school, he once brought home a report which said, "We had thought Hamish had reached rock bottom. But he has started digging."

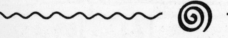

A technician was sent to Stornoway on the Isle of Lewis on a month's contract. He arrived on a grey, cloudy, drizzling day. He woke up next morning to find it was grey, cloudy, drizzling. The next day was the same, and the next. On the day after that, as he came out of his lodgings to find it was grey, cloudy and drizzling, he saw a small boy passing and said in exasperation, "Does the weather here ever change?"

"I don't know," said the child. "I'm only six."

A bank manager in rural Aberdeenshire went out to visit a farmer. When they had done their business, he was taken on a tour of the farm-yard. In a pig pen he saw a large white pig with a wooden hind leg.

"That's the bravest, most intelligent pig in the world," said the farmer.

"What happened to it?" asked the bank manager.

"Aye, weel," said the farmer, "there was a fire, ye see."

"In the yard?"

"No, no. In the hoose. The hoose went on fire one night when we were every one of us fast asleep. The pig jumped over the wall and broke in through the back door to tell us. I woke up with his feet on the bed. A brave pig!"

"Was he injured in the fire?"

"No, no. He went back inside again and dragged oot the bairns, all three of them, with his teeth."

"What a marvellous animal."

"Aye," said the farmer. "We owe our lives to that pig. There's not a finer pig in all the land."

"But how did he get the wooden leg?"

"Ach well," said the farmer, "if you have a pig of this quality, you don't eat him all at once as if he was some common animal."

When God created Scotland, He looked down on it with great satisfaction. Finally He called the Archangel Gabriel to have a look.

"Just see," said God. "This is the best yet. Splendid mountains, beautiful scenery, brave men, fine women, nice cool weather. And I've given them beautiful music and a special drink called whisky. Try some."

Gabriel took an appreciative sip.

"Excellent," he said. "But haven't you perhaps been too kind to them? Won't they be spoiled by all these things? Should there not be some drawback?"

"Just wait till you see the neighbours they're getting," said God.

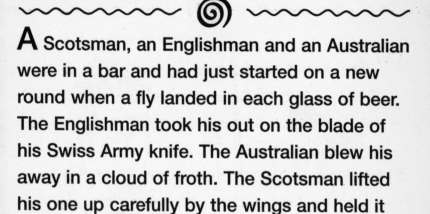

A Scotsman, an Englishman and an Australian were in a bar and had just started on a new round when a fly landed in each glass of beer. The Englishman took his out on the blade of his Swiss Army knife. The Australian blew his away in a cloud of froth. The Scotsman lifted his one up carefully by the wings and held it above his glass.

"Go on, spit it oot, ye wee devil," he growled.

The pretty Sunday School teacher asked her class, "How many of you want to go to Heaven?"

They all put up a hand except Tommy Mutch.

"Don't you want to go to Heaven, Tommy?" she asked.

"I can't go, Miss," he said. "Ma said I was to come straight home or I'd get a licking."

Jim had had a bad day fishing on the river and caught nothing. On the way home, he called in at the fish shop.

"Just throw me a small salmon," he said.

"Why throw it?" asked the fishmonger.

"So that I can tell my wife I caught it."

"Wouldn't you rather have a sea trout?"

"Why would I?" asked Jim.

"Well, when your wife came in earlier, she said that's what she'd prefer you to catch when you came in."

Charlie Maclean, the life insurance salesman, had a special way of getting reluctant customers to sign on the dotted line.

"Take your time, take your time," he would say. "Don't let me hurry you. Sleep on it, and if you wake up in the morning, let me know then."

Hector and Hamish were taken on by a company putting up telegraph poles. When they came back to the depot at the end of the first day, the foreman asked how many poles they had put up.

"Two," said Hamish proudly.

"Two?" spluttered the foreman. "The other squad have put in thirty."

"Maybe," said Hector, "But I bet they left them sticking away up out of the ground."

"Are you washed yet?" said the mother to her young son, after he had been in the bath for an hour.

"Oh, Ma, there's no soap."

"Haven't you got a tongue in your head?"

"Yes, but it can't reach the back of my neck."

When Old MacPherson celebrated his 95th birthday, his cronies, for a joke, sent him round an attractive young masseuse. When she rang the doorbell, he hobbled to answer and found himself gazing at the svelte blonde figure.

"I'm here to give you super sex," she said brightly. He thought for a minute.

"I'll ha'e the soup," he said finally.

Not everyone in Kittybrewster was pleased when the bus fares into central Aberdeen went down.

"Now I need to walk into town twice instead of only once to save a pound," mourned an active elderly resident.

A visitor to Edinburgh had lunch in a restaurant and left three pence on the table as a tip. As he left, he heard the waitress murmur something. He swung round.

"What did you say?" he asked.

She replied, "I was just saying you can tell a lot about a man by the tip he leaves."

"Oh, yes? And what can you tell about me?"

"I can tell three things about you straight off."

"Tell me then," said the visitor.

"Well, you're thrifty."

"That's true enough," said the man, pleased.

"And you're a bachelor."

"Yes, that's true too. And what's the third?"

"Your father was one too,"
said the waitress,
retreating to the kitchen.

Two robbers broke into a Glasgow lodging house. Once they were inside, a tremendous fight ensued. Bruised and bleeding, they finally emerged by the back window.

"We didnae do so bad," said one. "We came oot wi' twenty pounds."

"Aye," said the other. "But we went in wi' fifty."

The new minister came up into the pulpit with a jug of water and a glass and set them by the Bible. He was the kind of preacher who shouts and waves his arms about a lot. In the course of the sermon he drank up all the water in the jug.

"What did you think of him?" asked someone of the oldest member of the congregation afterwards.

"What did I think? Miraculous, just. The first windmill driven by water that I've ever seen."

Old Angus was taken to hospital with splinters of glass in his tongue.

"How did it happen?" asked the nurse.

Angus's tongue was too full of splinters for him to explain. Helpfully, the nurse gave him a pencil and a sheet of paper. He wrote:

"I dropped a bottle of whisky on the kitchen floor."

A Scotsman was on a visit to New York and decided to get his hair cut. Seeing a barber's salon, he went in.

"How much is a haircut?" he asked.

"Haircuts start at twenty dollars," he was told.

He rubbed his chin.

"How much is a shave?"

"A shave? Oh, a shave's ten dollars."

"Shave my head then," said the visitor.

A howling baby was causing a great disturbance in the supermarket. A lady shopper saw that the child was being pushed in a trolley by a small man who kept murmuring,

"It's okay, wee Jockie, just keep quiet. It'll be all right. Don't worry, don't lose your head. Keep calm, wee Jockie, keep calm."

The lady was impressed and said, "It's a shame wee Jockie isn't being quieter when you're being so good with him."

The man looked at her indignantly.

"What do you mean?" he said. "His name is Donald. I'm wee Jockie."

Old Wattie, a notorious poacher who had recently been fined for netting salmon, had promised to reform and had even joined the church. He was walking down the street with one of the elders when they encountered the local police sergeant.

"Well, Wattie," said the sergeant, "I'm glad to see you in good company. So you're not after the salmon any more?"

"No way," said Wattie.

"Or the deer?"

"No, sir, absolutely not."

"Very good, very good, keep up the good work," said the sergeant, and went on his way. Wattie turned to his companion and heaved a great sigh of relief.

"Man!" he said. "If he'd mentioned pheasants, I would have been in a real difficult position."

One of the Edinburgh scientists who cloned a sheep decided secretly to create a duplicate of himself by cloning. He did so, but to his great surprise, his clone, though exactly like him in every other way, would only speak in the most depraved and obscene language. Not only could he not take him anywhere in public, people mistook the clone for him, and he was asked to resign from the golf club and the scientists' lunch club. In despair, he lured his clone up to Fort William. They climbed Ben Nevis and he pushed his clone off the summit to his death. Unfortunately, he was seen doing the deed and the police came for him. In vain he protested that it was his own creation he had disposed of.

"No, sir," said the policeman. "It's a serious offence. We're arresting you for making an obscene clone fall."

A visitor to the Isle of Mull lost his way in the mist and wandered about the squelching mountainside for three days. At last the mist lifted slightly and in the distance he saw a man striding along with a shepherd's crook in his hand.

"Help, help," he called.

The man waited for him to come stumbling along.

"What's the maitter?" he asked.

"I'm lost," said the visitor pitifully. "I've been lost for three days."

"Is there a reward out for ye, do you think?" asked the local.

"Oh, I shouldn't think so."

"Well, ye're still lost," said the local, and walked off into the mist.

An elderly Scottish couple had just learned that they had won £22,000,000 in the National Lottery. Overwhelmed by their luck, they discussed what to do.

"I'm going to buy the bingo hall," said the woman, "so that all the old folks can play for nothing."

"And I'll buy the chippie," said her husband. "They can all come out and get a free fish supper."

"Yes, and I'll buy the bus company," said she, "so that they can all travel home free."

Her husband suddenly stood up.

"Put your coat on, Madge," he said.

"What's the matter, John? Where are you going?" she asked.

"We'd better get round to the bingo hall. When news of this gets about there's going to be a queue a mile long and we'll never get in."

The last Hamish and Hector story. Hamish and Hector went on a parachuting course. When they went up in the plane, Hamish jumped first, pulled his cord after ten seconds and began to float down. Then Hector jumped. He pulled his cord and nothing happened. He pulled the emergency cord. Nothing happened. In a moment he overtook Hamish as he plummeted down.

"Oh," called Hamish, "so we're racing, are we?" and ripped off his own 'chute harness.

This book is due for return on or before the last date shown below.

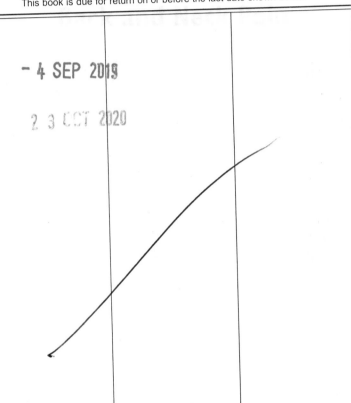